I0472904

Realities of Money

Be Alert and Be Wise

Kalyan Chary Edlore

This book is definitely not intended to highlight any person, place or thing, nor to criticize or hurt anyone's feelings or way of living. It is just an act of opinion sharing about the realities that the money can bring in one's life.

Introduction

MONEY, probably, the most powerful five letter word, is ruling the world today.

What is money superficially?

Money is an inert piece of paper or coin. It cannot talk and walk; it cannot see and hear, nor it can think and understand. Yet it is ruling the minds of crores of people. Almost everyone would list it as the first priority goal of life. But Why? One simple answer would be no one can imagine to lead a life without Money. Yes, it's perfectly true.

This inert but highly powerful substance called "Money" influences people in many different ways. In this book, based on my knowledge and observation, I have tried to showcase how money influences to become a good or bad person. I have discussed both pros and possible cons of having excess money in my own limited way.

I am writing this book out of deep concern on how many people are earning surplus money with lot of hard work but unable to spend rightfully and purposefully.

There are lots of people who take unnecessary stress and invest lot more time and effort to earn with the feeling that they may not earn sufficiently by working normally. I hope my opinions shared through this book help in a positive way.

This is a short and interesting book where my opinions about the nature of money are shared precisely and as clearly as possible.

Contents

Chapter No.	Chapter Name	Page No.
1	Money: Its Purpose and Importance	1
2	Money and its perceptions	4
3	Prepare, then Earn	6
4	Good things that money brings	8
5	Possible Bad effects of Money	18
6	Self-Assessment	25
7	Individual and Society are Interdependent	27
8	Do you have Surplus Money? Then What's next	29
9	My Personal Experience	31
10	Parent's Role towards their Children	32
11	Conclusion	34

Chapter 1

Money: Its Purpose and Importance

If you ask anyone, "Do you require Money? ", In high Probability the answer would a resounding "YES", After answering, he /she would conclude it to be a senseless question. Yes, it is really a senseless question. It is so obvious that everyone in this world require money for various reasons for the survival.

What is the purpose of money?

Why does one require money?

Is there anyone who doesn't understand the purpose of money?

With the exception of newly borne babies, everyone else has an understanding of how important the money's role is in one's life. Primary school children know that the school uniforms that they wear for going to school, the text books they read, the toys they use to play, and the chocolates, candies, and the ice creams they eat and enjoy come from money.

1

Money, most importantly, fulfils everyone's basic requirements of life, that is, Food, Clothing and Shelter. It is essential for all the purchases that one needs to make for the survival. Right from purchasing the daily bread to going on a luxurious vacation, money is required. In fact, money can be treated as second oxygen for our survival. It is a major contributor of happiness in anyone's life.

Money is so powerful in today's modern world, that about three fourths of one's lifetime is utilized in the process of earning it. But Money alone cannot give all the happiness in this world.

Agreed, Money is very powerful thing in this world. But, just like a coin has two faces, money too influences a person in two different ways. Hence one needs to be alert and be wise while choosing the path of earning and also while deciding to spend or invest the earned money.

In this new age, the amount of respect a person gets majorly depends on how much money the person has earned. A rich man, most often, gets higher respect compared to a poor man. Money plays a vital role is making someone more respectable. This is an unfortunate situation that the world is witnessing today. Ideally, a person should be respected based on the good virtues

and the good deeds that one is doing currently, or has already done good to the society in the past. In the recent times, one can find a lot of places where names of top rich people are published but there is hardly any place where names of top 'good' people are listed.

Chapter 2

Money and its perceptions

Does everyone perceive money in exactly the same manner?

The answer is 'No'. Money is perceived by people in different ways. This could be surprising for few people. But, yes, in my opinion it is very true.

A question may arise how is this possible?

Initially, when there is little money or less than sufficient income, it becomes the top most priority for every person. Most of the time in a day is invested in earning money and spending carefully and saving, wherever possible. Money takes most important place in one's life.

Once there is more than sufficient money to lead a financially comfortable life, the perception on money changes. Though many people still want to continue earning more and more income for their own personal expenses and savings, there are few people who have a totally different perception after reaching this stage. They feel completely protected in terms of their expenses and savings for life. At this

4

stage, Money is not the top most priority. People with this type of perception take up some philanthropic activities while they continue to earn with a goal to get a good name and fame in the society. A few others feel very happy and satisfied just by seeing someone whom they have helped happy.

They are few more rich people who want to lead a peaceful life with the earnings they made. They stop working and live with what they have earned. They prefer to keep the word 'Philanthropy' far from themselves.

People take different decisions in life depending upon how they perceive money after earning sufficiently to lead a happy life.

Chapter 3

Prepare, then Earn

It is very clear that money is required by everyone to lead a happy life. Not everyone makes career plans to earn money. While, some have well defined financial goals on how to earn and how much to earn, there are others who start earning money without having any financial goals and career plans in their mind.

Earning money is a fantastic feeling. But there is something that everyone needs to clearly understand before starting to earn money.

Before starting the process of earning money, it is worth having the knowledge about the impact that money can make on people's life in terms of changing one's ideas, ambitions, priorities, behaviour towards others, how the way of perceiving things change etc. It is very important to know that just like a coin has two sides, head and tail, money can impact in both positive and negative directions.

Just like it is necessary to gather proper information on the effects and the possible side

6

effects before purchasing a particular medicine and consuming it, it is very important to have a proper understanding of pros and possible cons of making money and becoming a rich person.

Knowing the nature of money gives an opportunity to prevent the possible loss that might occur due its negative influence.

Be aware of nature of Money right before you start earning it

Chapter 4

Good things that money brings

On the positive side, money increases the purchasing power. More the money one earns, more the purchasing power one gets. Apart from buying the basic needs, one can use money to buy or improve the amenities like better or bigger home, costly car etc. It gives lot of freedom to add other physical comforts at home. One can buy a better health policy and get sufficiently insured. More importantly, one can handle emergencies, if any, well and save more for the post retirement expenses.

Having sufficient money gives lot of self-confidence. It relieves stress levels and makes a person happier and motivates to work harder to get more success in life.

Positive effects of money can be discussed clearly based upon whether one is earning little money or sufficiently earning or earning more than sufficiently.

<u>When one is earning Little Money</u>

Being poor is a tough situation in life. Anyone would require money to manage basic necessities of life like food, clothing and shelter. Apart from these basic ones, one requires money for buying many products and services like transport, medicines etc. When one is poor and struggling to manage daily expenses, many situations arise where one is forced to compromise on the desires and manage the life depending on the money available. For example, if there is a desire to purchase a costly dress, and if there is no enough money to purchase that dress, then one has compromise by buying a dress sold at a cheaper price.

In this situation, a person becomes more serious about life. He starts thinking with more focus on how to earn and lead a happy life.

This situation of being a poor man gives an opportunity to learn lot of good lessons of life. One understands how much money is required to manage life. It will teach how to manage expenses effectively with little income. It will help in controlling the desires to spend on unnecessary or not-so-important things. This financial situation forces a person to work

9

harder and more efficiently. It will make person to search for better opportunities to make more income.

The situation where there is little income forces a poor man towards debts for certain important needs like education of children, health issues or any other financial emergency.

Most of the times banks do not give loans for a person who do not earn enough, as they do not get the confidence that a poor man would repay the complete loan amount along with the interest.

Even relatives and friends might not help for the same reason. Few lucky ones will have friends and relatives who are helpful in emergency situations.

When a person is poor, due to want of money, there is always a risk of getting into illegal activities like robbery, fraud etc.

This is the stage where one's mental strength is tested to the maximum. One needs to show lot of will power, patience, perseverance and courage in controlling the negative thoughts that are created within the mind and stick to the righteous way of earning.

10

<u>When one has sufficient income</u>

Money brings lot of good things. It is undoubtedly the major contributor of one's happiness. If one is earning sufficient money then it is a very good news.

It is well known fact that health is the real wealth. It is very important for everyone to lead a peaceful and happy life. Hence one should give high priority is maintaining a proper health. By earning sufficiently, one can invest on maintaining good health. Taking balanced diet and exercising regularly keeps one fit and healthy. One can join a gym for regularly workouts. One can even hire a trainer to help in the workouts. Another good practice is to go for regular health check-ups to make sure everything is fine.

If one earns crores but there is no proper health to enjoy and lead a happy life with that money, then what is use of earning those crores of money. Hence one should never overlook any health issues.

Talking about balanced diet, it is very important to understand what exactly is a balanced diet. Is it only the food which we eat in breakfast,

11

lunch and dinner? Definitely the answer is 'No'. All the thoughts that one gets in the mind can also be considered as food. Thoughts are food for the mind. So, it is very important to have positive thoughts in mind to keep away the stress. The reason is simple, Physical health depends on mental health. And stress strongly disturbs the mental health of a person. Earning sufficiently gives a person a good opportunity to lead a life without much stress.

It gives better living standards. One can afford to buy better living requirements such as a good house, an expensive car, a good insurance coverage for oneself and family.

Earning sufficiently gives an opportunity to invest in passive income generating businesses. Generating passive income sources gives an opportunity to earn income by investing few hours in a week.

Earning sufficiently gives opportunity to save. With proper financial planning one can invest in appropriate financial products based on risk-taking ability and targeted income, and save little by little, over a period of time. These savings can be used for various other necessities or as a post retirement fund.

12

One can maintain proper work life balance if there is sufficient and regular income.

Unlike good olden days where education was affordable even to a poor man, Education has become very expensive in the last few years. As parents aspire for the success of their children, they do not mind to spend money on their children's education even though it is a burden to them considering their income levels. Most of the parents who earn low to medium level depend on the education loans to provide quality education to their children at better schools and colleges. Having sufficient money allows parents to give an opportunity to their children to study in top colleges and universities without having any financial burden or with easily manageable financial burden.

Many low earning people have financial problems. Hence, they depend on debts to fulfil some of their specific needs. But people having a regular income can be away from the financial troubles, debts and the mental stress that these troubles and debts bring along.

Life these days is becoming more and more stressful due to multiple tasks that one has to perform parallelly and also by giving due respect to the time deadlines. Hence anyone would want to take a break from the busy schedule of daily life. A poor man can hardly afford a vacation for himself and family. But a person with sufficient income can take the family for a nice vacation, once in every three to six months, if not frequently.

When you have surplus income

Having surplus money is a boon. This financial state is something almost everyone aspires to be. A person with surplus money can do everything and much more than that is discussed in the previous section under the topic 'when you have sufficient money".

It takes lot of hard work to succeed and become a rich man. A few of them who have good luck will get into the list of rich men with comparatively lesser amount of hard work.

A person with surplus money, can invest money in new business initiatives, like financial markets or in fixed assets like big house, farm,

14

real estate property or similar valuable assets. Surplus money gives a person more opportunity to choose what he wants. For example, he can choose a desired place where he wants to live and construct a house of his liking. There will be more freedom to decide the cost, size, design and architecture, building contractor for the house.

A lot of talented people aspire to become wealthy by earning more money through business. But, unfortunately, they cannot manage to accumulate the money to fund their business start-up as they are poor. But this is not the case with the rich people with the surplus money. They can invest required money in business of their choice.

Maintaining a healthy body and a healthy mind is vital to every person life. One should be always fit and free from disease. Being fit and healthy not only gives energy to do our work but also encourages others to be fit. In this process, one can avoid becoming a dependent on family and friends. This, indirectly, is a favour to the family and friends where they are not put to hardships in supporting an unfit /diseased individual. Having

15

surplus money gives more opportunity to be fit where one can eat wholesome food regularly, that would have all the essential nutrients, like vitamins, minerals, Proteins, fibre etc. which are required for maintaining a healthy body. One can also take additional supplements, if required. As a practice, it is better to go for regular health check-ups just to make sure everything is perfectly fine with the body. There will be no problems to spend on regular check-ups for a rich person.

Over last few years, the world has seen a rapid increase in the pollution of the air, consequently increasing the chances of one becoming sick. Hence a comprehensive health insurance is unavoidable these days. It is a well-known fact that, good insurance companies charge high premiums to provide a good insurance coverage. Premium cost will further increase if one chooses to purchase the coverage for entire family. Having Surplus money gives more freedom to choose the best from the available lot in the market.

Having surplus money, gives an opportunity to lead a life which most of the young boys and girls aspire to get, namely, life with luxury. Yes, one can lead a luxurious and most comfortable life with good social status.

In this situation, where one has rightfully earned surplus income, would always be comfortable financially. Apart from himself, one can contribute in the happiness of entire family, friends and relatives wherever necessary.

There are many generous people who, out of their love and concern towards society, voluntarily come forward to serve the society. I salute, with all my heart, to such generous people. Surplus money gives a chance to put generosity in action. As there are lot of kind hearted people in the world but unfortunately, they don't have enough money to contribute to the philanthropic activities. Rich and generous minded people can undertake philanthropic activities without much hesitation and contribute in the welfare of the society.

17

Chapter 5

Possible Bad effects of Money

Having discussed the beneficial effects of money in the previous chapters, let's proceed to understand the other side of money, that is the possible negative influences that the money can bring to one's life.

Now, Money, which everyone likes, can get someone into lot of troubles which can make the person reach to a very low level in society.

Following are some of the important bad consequences one can face if there is no proper check on the method or process of earning money and on the purpose for which money being spent:

1) **_Money Mindedness_** – The luxurious comforts that the Money provides can make a person more and more greedy and can change a person into completely 'Money Minded' and consequently can make him take a wrong investment decision and face a financial loss.

Money minded people always make plans to earn more money but fail to balance the

18

professional life with their family life. There is a huge risk of creating a disconnect within family members if this particular issue is neglected.

2) **_Motivates Unlawful deeds_** -The benefits of money lures many people towards unlawful and non- righteous activities like Corruption, Robbery, Financial Scams etc. World has seen lot of people being punished by law for involving into these unlawful activities since long time. There is one single motive behind doing these kinds of activities, that is, MONEY. Excessive desire to earn more money influences a people to take wrong steps (unlawful deeds). If done repeatedly, it becomes a bad habit and ruins one's life.

3) **_Excessive unhealthy habits_** -Lots of surplus money can influence in a negative way. It can make the people habituated to too much of lavish living, Excessive alcoholism, Tobacco, drugs and other unhealthy habits. Once lavish living becomes a habit, it is difficult to come out of it which consequently results in the degradation of the health, wealth and prosperity.

4) **_Property Disputes_** -There are lot of families where the excessive desire for money has

19

created differences among the family members with regard to property matters. Most of the times, the loving and caring relationships that one has maintained with parents, brothers and sisters within the family, over many years, break once the property disputes come in.

5) **_Degradation of Moral Values_** – In the olden days, Majority of people used to give lot of importance to the moral values. People used to live happily with whatever little money they could earn by following moral values, namely, Truth, honesty, righteousness, and non-violence. Though, they worked harder and earned more income but never compromised on the moral values as they knew the value of following these morals.

Where are these moral values today? Well, I should say, they are only seen in the printed formats in text books and religious texts. Day by day, the percentage of honest and truthful persons is degrading. If one analyses the reasons, with an objective frame of mind, it is quite evident that the majority of people have changed their priority from "Moral Value" to "Money Value".

20

Not Following Morals values while earning money can have serious consequences. Non-righteous ways of earning money can change a rich person to Poor, a good gentleman to a bad man, and consequently from a happy man to a sad or depressed man.

6) ***Makes people Jealously:*** Jealously works with following attitude, *My friend or someone whom I know, has bought a new item so I also need to buy* - Jealously is one such bad habit, which generates strong push within the mind to buy things which others already bought even if they are not necessary or useful. More jealous individuals tend to spend a lot of money unnecessarily and fuel this bad habit within them. The purchasing power that the money brings is the culprit which indirectly influences an individual to nurture this bad habit, namely, jealousy.

7) ***Bigger Ego:*** Having more money one of the important factors that contributes highly to make a person more egoistic.

If someone has a doubt as to, what ego exactly is?

21

Ego is a feeling of self-importance and self-esteem.

Everyone has some amount of ego. The problem arises only when it crosses a threshold. A feeling that one is rich and he has become rich using his immense talent and capability makes a person's thinking impaired. It gives a feeling of self-importance in excess.

This ego makes a person change his behaviour towards his work, colleagues, family and friends. This makes the person lose his respect.

Just like a fearful person cannot think clearly on how to act in given situation, a person with ego cannot think clearly and consequently cannot make better decisions in difficult situations. He stops discussing the issues with the family and friends before taking any decisions on the issues.

8) **_Anger and Arrogance:_** One hardly gets an opportunity to see a person who never shows anger at others. Anger is a common bad quality that most of the people possess. But generally, one shows anger with a proper reason. But money can make a person show anger without a proper reason. It can make a person shout at

others without making proper analysis over the situation. It can make people show arrogance and talk disrespectfully and show their superiority.

9) _More Money, More Parties_: Most of the rich people tend to make a greater number of friends and contacts in the society. Consequently, they get more invitations for various parties. This makes a rich person to give more time for parties and less time to family.

They fail to understand the importance of spending time with family and children.

It is very important to spend productive time with family. It is especially important to give some relaxation to children from their hectic daily routine. They feel happy if they are taken to a picnic, resort or a good restaurant which serves tasty and favourite foods.

10) _More Money, More Technology_: In the recent times, world is more behind technology.

Generally, when the person grows financially, the number of electronic gadgets within the home tend to grow. While elders like to have multiple cell phones, children like to have multiple video games to play. So, there are television sets, mobiles, laptops, tablets, video games to keep all the people in family engaged. While parents get busy with official or personal calls on mobiles, Children get busy watching their favourite programs on television or play video games. This results in the family members spend most of their free time with electronic devices rather than spend some productive time with family members. This would be one of the important factors that contributes in creating disconnect between parents and children.

Chapter 6

Self-Assessment

In spite of earning sufficient money, many people feel that they still have to earn lot of money to lead a happy life. This, I think, basically comes out of lack of proper financial planning. This feeling can also come due to the income comparison that one makes with the friends and relatives.

If you ask anyone, "Do you have enough Money?", the answer, most of the times, would be undoubtedly, "No".

How much to earn? this is a most important question that needs to be answered.

How much money would make my life free from financial problems?

How much money would give me never ending comfort throughout my life, both to me and to my family?

Though it is very difficult to figure out how much money is actually required for one life due to uncertainties of life. There are some "Retirement Saving Calculators" available online for help. One can, if required, take the

25

help of a qualified and a trust worthy financial planner. A qualified financial Planner helps in meeting one's financial goals. Also, one can get an estimated amount required to lead a life which is financially comfortable.

If one is confident of earning this amount, then there is no point in leading a stressful life.

Chapter 7

Individual and Society are Interdependent

Before starting the topic on surplus money, it is very important to understand the role that the society plays in everyone's life.

Society and individuals (including animals and plants) are interdependent, there is no society without individuals and individuals cannot live without society.

One depends on society for almost everything. One depends on a teacher for education, doctor for a medical treatment, farmer for food etc. If thought deeply, one can easily understand and firmly believe that each and everything that one gets in life is from the society. So, in gratitude towards what one receives from the society, it is the duty of every individual to make positive and wholehearted effort to contribute for the welfare of society. How much to contribute and how to contribute is a decision that one needs to make for oneself.

World has hundreds of philanthropists who are contributing for the welfare of society. There are NGOs, Private companies who are doing charity work in their own way and contributing positively.

While there are few people who, out of their love towards fellowmen donate for the welfare of needy people in fulfilling the basic living requirements like food, shelter, education or medication.

There are few others who love animals and donate to facilitate better living conditions for animals.

There are some more generous hearts who have lot of affection on the environment and feel protecting environment is top priority. So, they go ahead and help in protecting nature by planting trees, etc.

Tons of appreciations to all those who out of their love towards fellow livings beings are ready to sacrifice a good percentage of their hard-earned money for the benefit of society. They are really blessed people.

In my opinion, God appreciates a life with gratitude.

Chapter 8

Do you have Surplus Money? Then What's next

There are lot of fortunate people around the world who, out of their hard work and blessings of God earn surplus money. But only few would have that brave and generous heart to spend that money for the welfare of the fellow men and other living beings like animals and plants.

For those who have surplus money and willing to spend towards welfare of society, I am listing few social welfare initiatives which would benefit society substantially,

1) Fund tree plantations for environment protection.

2) Fund advertisements aiming social welfare in social media.

3) Help Children get quality education.

4) Fund high quality health facilities to poor.

5) Use digital marketing services to create awareness on cleanliness.

29

6) Fund quality food for the poor on regular basis

Above listed initiatives are just few examples, it is up to one's decision on how to contribute for the welfare of the society.

Many times, almost entire lifetime is spent in earning money for one's living, but having surplus money gives time and mental peace to focus on the spiritual progress like reading religious books, visiting worship places and allocate time on meditation.

Chapter 9

My Personal Experience

There is a great amount of happiness one can derive by helping the needy.

Here I want to share my personal experience as an example:

There are lot of pigeons around my home. Few weeks back, while I was watching them fly in the sky, I doubted if these pigeons are getting enough food daily. So, I decided to help these birds by giving them some food every day. I started giving some cereals and rice to them every afternoon. I feel very happy when these birds come and eat the food given by me.

Chapter 10

Parent's Role towards their Children

Parents play a very important role in making children understand the role of money in one's life. Children understand the value and use of money. Many start making career plans and set financial goals right from the time when they are in teenage. So, it is important that they understand the nature of money when they are young.

 Many parents give some pocket money to children on daily basis but they fail to track on how the children are spending this pocket money. The reason could be the over confidence that they have on the children where they believe that children would never misuse the given money, or they are so busy that they miss on this crucial point. For any reason, children should not be at loss.

 I think, Children within the age group of 12-20 years are more at risk as this is the age when goals, beliefs, habits, impressions get into their minds. So, it is the duty of each parent to educate their children on the do's and don'ts of money.

It is also the duty of teachers in the high school and college to make the children take matured decisions with respect to spending the hard-earned money of the parents.

Having good friends at school and college is most important point as the company of good friends makes a lot of positive impact on the children's personality. Parents also should explain the importance of making good friends at school/ college.

Children after a particular age, start observing the habits of the parents. They observe how parents are earning and spending money. Parents who have good income earning, spending and saving habits can influence their children's mindset in a positive manner.

Parents, if required, can consult financial planners for getting a suitable risk-based investment advice.

Chapter 11

Conclusion

This process of gaining knowledge and preparing oneself for the challenge of earning money starts right from age three or age four when one joins school in the childhood as a kinder-garden student.

After completing education after years of hard work in schools and colleges, and gaining additional skills, one gains knowledge, confidence and opportunity to earn. Having invested a lot of time and money to acquire education and necessary skill sets to master in a particular field, everyone would want to make maximum use of their talent by utilizing the opportunities that come along, whether in an employment or business.

It is a well-known fact that it requires a good amount of hard work to earn money.

Having earned a lot of money by using acquired talent and investing time and money, it is very important to know how to make right use of the acquired income for one's own progress and for the progress of family and society, if possible.

Having financial goals is very much appreciated. Achieving them is a thrill and gives lot of satisfaction. But one has to be well aware of the possible imbalances that money can bring in one's truthfulness, overall commitments, personal relationships and obligations in the long run.

Money is like fire, if one is careful while using, it will work as intended but if one is careless then it will burn the fingers.

No one can stop anyone from being happy. As each person's happiness is within his mind. If one is satisfied with what he gets then happiness is always in the mind. It doesn't mean that one should not aim at earning more but a happy and peaceful mind can make better and faster decisions in life, as compared to unsatisfied and stressed one.

Feeling that only money gives happiness is completely incorrect. Money is definitely important to fulfil certain unavoidable needs in the journey of life, but importance on earning money beyond a point can be harmful. If

35

surplus money comes the right way, it's fantastic, else if it doesn't then still fine. It is not the end of world. One can still live happily even by earning sufficiently.

Parents, teachers, guardians and friends should share the responsibility of educating children about the right way of earning and using money.

One should always have self-confidence and positive thinking about one's success in life.

Finally, I would like to conclude this book by sharing this one important opinion... One should earn money to live a happy life and should not live only to earn money. One should not become a slave in the hands of money. Be alert and Be wise.

I thank you so much for investing your valuable time and money on my book.

36